FAT LOSS FOR THE REAL WORLD

Lose Fat And Keep It Off Without Restrictive Diets, Food Guilt, Or Workouts You Hate

By **Lester Kitching**

Get Your **FREE** Fat Loss Toolkit At: **LesterKitching.com/ToolKit**

Copyright © 2025 Lester Kitching

All rights reserved.

No part of this publication may be reproduced, distributed, or transmitted in any form or by any means, including photocopying, recording, or other electronic or mechanical methods, without the prior written permission of the publisher.

Printed in the United Kingdom by Amazon KDP

This book is for general educational purposes only. It is not medical advice and shouldn't replace guidance from a qualified healthcare professional.

Always consult your GP or another healthcare professional before changing your diet, exercise, or lifestyle - especially if you have any existing medical conditions and injuries. If at any point you feel unwell when following the guidance in this book, or think you may have an eating disorder or another health condition, consult a medical professional immediately.

The author and publisher accept no responsibility for any loss, injury, or damage that may occur as a result of following the information in this book.

ISBN: 9798273172029

Get Your **FREE** Fat Loss Toolkit At: [**LesterKitching.com/ToolKit**](https://LesterKitching.com/ToolKit)

Get Your **FREE** Fat Loss Toolkit At: **LesterKitching.com/ToolKit**

CONTENTS

Introduction..15

PART 1

The Foundations...21

    Why This Book Is Different...................................22

    Focus On What Really Matters............................23

    High Impact, Not Total Overhaul.........................25

    This Book Is Built For You.......................................26

PART 2

The Transformation Framework........................27

    Phase 1: Ignite (0–90 Days)...................................29

    Phase 2: Momentum (3-6 Months)...................30

    Phase 3: Identity (6 Months Onwards)............32

    Where Most People Go Wrong...........................34

Get Your **FREE** Fat Loss Toolkit At: LesterKitching.com/ToolKit

PART 3

The Transformation System..................37

Build A Powerful Vision..........................41

Nutrition Simplified.................................51

Training That Fits Real Life....................81

Unstoppable Mindset.............................95

The Power Of Sleep..............................111

The Fallback Protocol...........................117

The Real Reason You'll Stick To It......125

PART 4

This Time Really Is Different................131

Final Words..135

Get Your **FREE** Fat Loss Toolkit At: **LesterKitching.com/ToolKit**

Get Your **FREE** Fat Loss Toolkit At: **LesterKitching.com/ToolKit**

Download Your Fat Loss For The Real World Toolkit

To help you implement what you learn in this book, you can download a free toolkit which has a collection of helpful, practical resources.

Inside, you'll find tools to help you:

- **Set clear, meaningful goals** that actually keep you motivated.

- **Plan meals with confidence** so you can eat well without stress, guilt, or restriction.

- **Train efficiently** with workouts that fit around work, family, and real life - not the other way around.

- **Stay consistent** even when life gets messy or motivation dips.

- **Build the mindset and structure** that makes this time the one that lasts.

These are tools I use with my clients every day - and they're designed to make your fat loss journey simpler, smoother, and far more enjoyable.

To download your free Fat Loss Toolkit, head to:

LesterKitching.com/Toolkit

Get Your **FREE** Fat Loss Toolkit At: <u>LesterKitching.com/ToolKit</u>

Get Your **FREE** Fat Loss Toolkit At: **LesterKitching.com/ToolKit**

For Your Consideration When You've Finished Reading The Book...

If you like what you read in this book, and you want to continue the journey, you're invited to one of my live educational workshops - hosted regularly both virtually and in-person.

Spaces are intentionally limited so you can share your experiences, ask questions, and get personalised coaching directly from me.

These are completely free to attend, so as you can imagine, they will fill up quickly.

To find out when and where the next educational workshops are taking place, head to:

LesterKitching.com/Workshop

or email **lester@lesterkitching.com**

Dedication

To **Emily, Sofia, and Harry**, you're my reminder of what truly matters every day.

You fill my life with love and fun - whether that's dance parties in the kitchen or super races in the garden - moments that remind me to slow down and enjoy life as it happens.

You've shaped the way I see health and fitness - as something that should enhance life, not take it over. I never want to miss out on the moments that matter most, and you're the reason *Fat Loss For The Real World* exists.

And to **Paul Gough**, who I've learned so much from over the last four years. Thank you for showing me what's possible, and for giving me the belief to make it happen. This book would not exist without your mentorship..

Foreword

I've been fortunate to work alongside many brilliant coaches over the years, and Lester is one of the most talented and genuine.

What makes Lester stand out is his ability to connect with people on a real level. He gets what it's like - the confusion, the overwhelm, the pressure people feel around fat loss and fitness.

I've seen him help countless clients by keeping things simple, real, and non-threatening. There's no ego, no complicated jargon, just honest advice that actually works.

In an industry full of noise and quick fixes, Lester's approach is refreshingly straightforward. He understands that people don't need extreme protocols or unrealistic promises - they need clarity, support, and a plan they can genuinely stick to while living their real lives.

This book reflects everything I admire about Lester's coaching: it's practical, compassionate, and built on helping real people get real results. If you're tired of the confusion and just want someone who genuinely gets it, you're in exactly the right hands.

Andrew Burton

Owner, Active Body Conditioning

Get Your **FREE** Fat Loss Toolkit At: LesterKitching.com/ToolKit

About The Author

Hi! My name is Lester, and first of all, I want to thank you and share my appreciation that you're reading this book. It is not lost on me that you are taking time out of your day, and before we get started, I wanted to tell you my back story so you understand a little bit more about who I am, and how I can help you.

I started my coaching journey in 2014 and spent almost three years training clients in person at a gym in Middlesbrough, in the North East of England.

In 2017, I stepped away from coaching full-time - but I never stopped training myself or helping friends and family who wanted to lose fat and feel more confident without spending all their time in the gym or obsessing over food.

Then in 2021, I married my amazing wife, Emily, and we've since had two children - Sofia (2022) and Harry (2024). Becoming a dad changed everything for me. Suddenly, I wasn't just a twenty-something with unlimited time and energy. I had real responsibilities, and like every parent, I wanted to show up for my kids with energy, set a positive example, and give them a happy childhood.

That completely changed what training and nutrition meant for me. It was no longer just about how I looked - it became about how I could be the best version of myself for my family. I wanted to train in a way that gave me energy, not exhaustion. I wanted to eat well, but simply. And above all, I wanted to spend more time with my family, not less.

I realised how I live sets the example my children will follow. I didn't want them growing up seeing obsessive dieting, guilt, or body shame as "normal." I know I can't protect them from everything, but I can give them a foundation - to know how to eat, move, and live healthily without extremes.

That mindset shaped everything in this book. It led me to identify and refine the principles that truly work in real life - the same ones that helped my most successful clients over the years.

I've spent many late nights writing this book, putting as much effort into what to leave out as what to include. My goal wasn't to write a textbook full of jargon or endless tactics - it was to create something simple, impactful, and practical. A guide that helps you achieve lasting fat loss without restriction, starvation, obsession, or hours in the gym doing workouts you hate.

So before you dive in, here's my final message:

If you feel like you've tried everything… even if you've struggled for years to lose fat, tone up, and feel confident again - **you can do it.**

You've just been following the wrong strategies - ones that work on good days, but fail on the bad ones.

Reading this book is your first step toward changing that - and I'm very excited to help you finally achieve what you've wanted for so long.

Get Your **FREE** Fat Loss Toolkit At: **LesterKitching.com/ToolKit**

Get Your **FREE** Fat Loss Toolkit At: LesterKitching.com/ToolKit

Introduction

Most people already know what to do to lose weight. You've read the articles, watched YouTube videos, and probably done a few plans that worked - for a while.

The problem isn't knowledge - it's consistency. Doing the right things long enough to see them work.

Life looks very different now than it did in your 20s. You've got bigger work commitments, family responsibilities, and social things you can't always skip. Sleep gets cut short, stress runs high, and there's always something (or someone) that needs your attention.

Then the unexpected hits - a work deadline, a weekend away, the kids come down with something - and the plan falls apart. You tell yourself you'll start again when things calm down. But they never really do.

That's the real reason most people struggle. Not because they're lazy or unmotivated, but because they've been trying to follow systems built for perfect weeks. The kind where your schedule's empty, motivation's high, and life behaves itself.

So when life gets messy - which it always will - the plan collapses. And every time that happens, it chips away at your belief that you can actually do this.

But it's not your fault.

Most plans expect life to fit the plan. This one fits the plan to your life.

Why This Book Is Different

When I started coaching in 2014, I noticed a pattern. People weren't failing because they didn't care. They were failing because their plan didn't allow them to be human.

They'd have a great few weeks, or even months - training well, eating better, feeling more in control - then something would throw them off.

It might have been a stressful week at work, a holiday that threw them out of routine, or a sick child. Whatever the reason, suddenly it felt like everything was undone.

So I built a different approach.

One that plans for chaos rather than pretending it doesn't exist. One that focuses on the few actions that drive most results. One that teaches you how to win the week - even when the conditions aren't perfect.

Over time, that approach evolved into two key parts:

- **The Transformation Framework:** a roadmap that shows what to expect and how to keep progressing at every stage of your fat loss journey.

- **The Transformation System:** the structure that simplifies training, nutrition, mindset, and accountability so you can finally get the results you've spent years trying and failing to achieve.

Together, they work when motivation dips and time is short - because that's when most plans fall apart.

What You'll Get From This Book

This isn't another quick-fix or "perfect plan". It's a roadmap designed for people who want lasting results - built around the way real life actually works.

No overhaul. No starvation. No gym obsession.

You just need to focus on the few things that deliver a huge portion of the results - consistently.

Along the way, you'll also see short sections highlighting **Common Mistakes to Avoid** and **What to Do Instead** - simple, practical takeaways that make it easy to remember and apply what really matters, without overthinking the details.

Here's how we'll do it:

- The Transformation Framework - the three phases, how you'll feel along the way, and how to navigate them.

- The Transformation System - train, eat, think, and stay accountable without guilt or grind

By the end, you'll have a simple structure that helps you lose fat, keep it off, and stay in control - because your plan bends, not breaks, on the bad weeks.

You don't need the stars to align.

You just need a structure that works in the real world.

Who This Book Is (And Isn't) For

This book isn't for everyone - and that's intentional.

If you're training for a bodybuilding show, chasing elite-level performance, or planning to take on an Ironman, you'll need a far more specialised and extreme approach than what's covered here.

Those goals demand greater sacrifice, and a level of discipline that most people - especially the parents, professionals, and those with busy lives I specialise in working with - simply don't have the time or desire for. And that's okay.

This book is for people who want to look great and feel confident **without sacrificing the rest of their life to do it.**

It's for you if you want to:

- Lose fat in a way that fits your real life and doesn't require you to obsess over nutrition or training.

- Have more energy for your kids, your career, and just feel happier in general.

- Feel confident in your clothes and proud of what you see in the mirror or when you head to the pool on holiday in your swimwear.

- Enjoy weekends, meals out, and family events without guilt or restriction.

You've got important goals - just not extreme ones.

And you want to make this simpler, more enjoyable way of exercising and eating a permanent part of your identity, but not the only part.

Real transformation doesn't require living like a full-time athlete. It comes from learning how to balance fat loss results with family, work, social events, and overall freedom and happiness in a way that lasts.

A Quick Note Before You Dive In

This book is designed to give you the *framework and understanding* behind real, lasting fat loss - not to bury you in every possible detail.

Throughout the chapters, you'll see short mentions of the **Transformation Toolkit** - a free set of practical resources to help you *apply* what you're learning.

Inside, you'll find tactical tools - training templates, nutrition planners, and self-review checklists - all built to save you time and make implementation simple.

You don't need to stop reading to grab them, but once you've finished the book, they'll be waiting for you here: LesterKitching.com/Toolkit

Think of this book as your roadmap - and the Toolkit as the gear that helps you travel it faster.

PART 1

The Foundations

The 80/20 Approach

Before we get into the roadmap, I want to make something very clear. This book isn't about obsessing over the tiny details that most people waste energy on. It's about the *big picture* and prioritising your focus and efforts on the handful of things that actually make a difference.

Most people fail because they try to major in minors.

They focus on all the wrong things:

- Back squats or leg presses.
- If they should eat breakfast or skip it.
- Which type of milk is best.

They overthink things that barely move the needle, while ignoring the simple foundations that make the biggest difference.

The problem with that approach? It burns through your willpower. You spend so much energy trying to be perfect that you run out of energy to stay consistent

That's where the 80/20 rule comes in.

80% of your results will come from 20% of your actions. The key is knowing which 20% matters most – then doing those things well, more often than not.

That's what this book is built around. Not hacks, not fads, not 'one secret food,' but clear, simple principles that work.

Get Your **FREE** Fat Loss Toolkit At: LesterKitching.com/ToolKit

Focus On What Really Matters

Most fitness advice lives at the low level - buried in the micro details. Things like rep ranges, macros, supplements, or which piece of kit to use.

The problem?

Those things are highly individual and short-lived.

For example, whether you choose a back squat, a hack squat, or a leg press depends on your body, your experience, your mobility, and what equipment you have access to.

And after a few months, you'll probably change exercises anyway - either because progress slows, or you just get bored.

The same goes for nutrition.

It doesn't matter whether you prefer rice, potatoes, or pasta - what matters is that your food choices *fit your life* while still achieving your fat loss goal and most importantly of all, you can keep doing them long term.

This book focuses on the structure that makes the small choices work.

Because when you understand the higher-level principles - how to train effectively, eat consistently, and stay accountable - the small stuff stops mattering so much.

You can adapt to any situation.

You can go on holiday, have a busy week, deal with family stress and still know exactly what to do.

That's what creates freedom.

It's not about being perfect. It's about being in control.

Common Mistakes To Avoid

Getting lost in the details before mastering the basics.

Most people start their fat loss journey buried in minutiae - arguing over carb timing, supplements, or the "best" exercise for abs - while ignoring the habits that actually move the needle. They chase complexity because it feels productive, but it only leads to confusion, burnout, and giving up when results stall.

What To Do Instead

Think high-level first - build the structure, then fine-tune later.

When you understand the big picture - eat in a calorie deficit, train hard a few times a week, move more, stay accountable - the rest becomes flexible. The details matter only once your foundations are consistent. Start with principles. Add tactics when they're needed, not before.

Get Your **FREE** Fat Loss Toolkit At: LesterKitching.com/ToolKit

High Impact, Not Total Overhaul

At the start of your transformation, your goal isn't to overhaul everything. It's to focus on the few most important things, nail them, and build from there.

If you try to completely change your diet, train five days a week, sleep eight hours a night, drink more water, meditate, and hit 10,000 steps all at once… you're setting yourself up for failure.

Not because you don't care - but because it's very difficult to juggle that many changes on top of real life.

That's why we start small - focusing on a handful of powerful priorities, building the highest-impact habits, and layering progress as you go.

Successful transformations follow a simple pattern:

1. Identify what will have the biggest impact
2. Do it consistently and ignore the other stuff
3. Add the next thing only when the first thing is solid

That's the opposite of what most plans teach - but it's exactly why it works.

Common Mistake To Avoid

Trying to change everything at once.

The "all-in Monday" approach feels exciting - new plan, new diet, new you - but that buzz fades fast when real life hits. Then, the gym sessions slip, the meal prep stops, and you're left feeling like you've failed again. The problem isn't motivation - it's the impossible load you've tried to carry all at once.

What To Do Instead

Start small, then layer success.

Pick one or two habits that will create the biggest impact, like tracking your meals and training twice per week. Master those, then build. Momentum comes from consistency, not chaos. The simpler the start, the stronger the foundation.

This Book Is Built For You

This book is built for people with real lives - people who can't hit pause on work, family, or social events just to "get in shape."

It's built for the person who's been stuck in that start-stop cycle for years and is finally ready for something that lasts.

If that's you, this book will finally make everything make sense - why you've struggled before, what's been missing, and how to make progress that actually sticks.

The next chapter is where it all starts - The Transformation Framework.

It's the roadmap that shows you what to expect at every stage, what most people feel, and how to stay on track even when motivation fades.

Let's get started…

PART 2

The Transformation Framework

The Transformation Framework

Every transformation happens in stages. You don't go from stuck to unstoppable overnight - it's a process that unfolds in phases.

The challenge is, most people have no idea what those phases actually look like. So when motivation dips or progress slows, they assume something's wrong with them. They panic, change everything (even if it was working), or quit completely.

Those moments are part of the process.

When you know what to expect, you can plan for it. You can prepare for the dips, slowdowns, and those moments where it feels like you're going backwards.

That's what the Transformation Framework does: it gives you a roadmap that predicts the journey.

It's broken into three stages:

- **Ignite (0 to 90 days)**
- **Momentum (3 to 6 months)**
- **Identity (6 months and beyond)**

Each stage brings its own challenges, emotions, and lessons. Most people experience similar things along the way - but how you respond determines your long-term success. That's what separates you from your former self who tried and failed without a plan that worked in the real world.

Get Your **FREE** Fat Loss Toolkit At: LesterKitching.com/ToolKit

Phase 1: Ignite (0–90 Days)

This is where everything begins. You're fired up. Motivation's high. You're ready to finally make this stick.

Most people feel a mix of excitement and overwhelm here. They want to change everything all at once - overhaul their food, train five days a week, cut out alcohol, and get "perfect".

But perfect doesn't last.

That's where most people slip. They go too hard, too fast, and burn out before real progress even starts.

You will hit moments in these first few weeks where it feels like too much. You'll question whether you can actually keep up. That's not failure - it's part of the process.

The key here is clarity, not intensity.

The Transformation System fixes this by giving you structure and direction so you know exactly what matters most, what to ignore, and how to get those early wins that build belief.

When you start with a short list of priorities and stack early wins, confidence grows fast.

That's the whole goal of Ignite: Start strong with clear targets that fit the real world and bank those early wins that build your confidence.

Common Mistake To Avoid

Trying to change everything all at once.

At the start, motivation tricks you into thinking more is better — new workouts, strict diets, no alcohol, early mornings, and full overhaul mode. It feels productive, but it's really just unsustainable pressure. Within weeks, life catches up, routines collapse, and you're back where you started, wondering why you can't "stay disciplined."

What To Do Instead

Start small and win early.

Pick one or two priorities that make the biggest impact - like nailing your weekday meals and getting three workouts done. Build momentum by doing less, better. Every small win stacks belief and creates proof that you *can* do this. Once the foundations feel automatic, then you layer more in.

Phase 2: Momentum (3–6 Months)

If you've made it through the first three months, this is where things often start to drift.

They've built good habits, seen results, and things are starting to click - but now the rate of change slows.

Most people feel frustrated here. They look in the mirror and see less change than before. Their peers are no longer the vocal cheerleaders they once were at the start of the journey. The novelty wears off too - especially if workouts aren't enjoyable and nutrition feels restrictive.

Progress will slow down, and you'll have days where motivation dips or boredom creeps in. It's completely normal - but it's important to keep building the momentum, rather than letting yourself slide back into old habits, which ultimately lead to you undoing your progress so far.

People often quit here not because it isn't working, but because they expect linear progress and the same excitement as they felt in the first week.

Accountability, variety, and perspective solve this.

That structure keeps your focus on the bigger picture - so when motivation drops, the plan still carries you forward.

This phase is where consistency compounds. Your small actions - the ones that once felt insignificant - start to pay off in ways you can't always see day to day.

Momentum is about trust: in the process, in the structure, and in yourself. Progress is still happening, even when it slows down.

Common Mistake To Avoid

Expecting constant progress and excitement.

This is the stage where many people get restless. They mistake slower progress for failure, start changing plans, chasing quick fixes, or dropping habits that were actually working. They forget that plateaus are part of progress - not proof it's stopped.

What To Do Instead

Double down on consistency and perspective.

Progress isn't always visible week to week, but it's happening under the surface. Keep showing up, keep tracking, and keep refining. Use accountability to stay focused and let structure replace motivation when it dips. Remember - this is where the long-term transformers separate themselves.

Phase 3: Identity (6+ Months)

You've made huge progress by this stage. You're fitter, lighter, stronger, and you feel more in control. You may have even reached your original goal.

But now, a new challenge appears - staying there.

Most people feel proud but uncertain at this point. They've hit their initial goal, and without a clear next step, the actions that got them here start to fade.

You will be tempted to ease off.

To train less, relax your food, or think "I can take it easier now".

That's human nature - but it's also why so many people slide backwards. And I know how devastating it feels to work for months toward a body you're proud of, only to regress back to where you started.

That's difficult to handle, and if you've experienced this before, I understand how tough it is.

The Transformation System fixes this by evolving with you. In the beginning, you needed more structure and guidance.

Now, you've built your confidence in the gym, you have found a groove with eating in a way you enjoy, and you need light-touch accountability - check-ins, goals, and refinement.

The focus shifts from "getting results" to keeping them effortlessly - and, if you choose, setting a new goal.

That's the moment your identity changes.

You're no longer trying to get in shape - you simply live that way now.

And that's the ultimate goal.

Because when you reach it, you will have achieved something you've most likely spent countless hours (and a lot of money) working towards in all your previous attempts.

And the best bit?

By following the Transformation System, you're no longer getting overwhelmed with exercise, feeling shame over food choices, or hiding under baggy clothes.

Common Mistake To Avoid

Easing off too much once you've "made it."

After months of effort, it's tempting to relax - fewer workouts, less tracking, more flexibility. But without structure, those small slips compound. The habits that got you here start to fade, and before you realise it, you're undoing months of progress.

What To Do Instead

Evolve your structure, don't erase it.

Shift from full structure to light-touch accountability - monthly check-ins, mini goals, and small refinements. Keep the habits that built your results but make them fit your new lifestyle. You're not "on a plan" anymore - you're living the identity you've built.

Where Most People Go Wrong

Most people never make it past Ignite. They throw everything at it, which is noble, but also a path to failure.

They burn out, stop, start again later, and repeat the cycle.

Each time, they get more confused, frustrated, and doubtful that they'll ever reach their goal.

The few who reach Momentum often stall there - frustrated as progress inevitably slows and distracted from the things that were working.

And even fewer can navigate Identity, because they remove the very thing that got them results in the first place - accountability and structure.

This Transformation Framework stops that pattern by showing you where you are, and what comes next.

The next chapter, The Transformation System, is where we take this roadmap and give it structure.

It's the method that makes the Framework work in real life.

PART 3

The Transformation System

The Transformation System

Now we'll build the engine that drives everything forward. This is where the roadmap turns into daily action that actually fits your life.

The Transformation System is how we take the concepts and make them work in your life.

It's built around **seven key pillars** that cover everything you need to make change stick:

1. **Goal Setting** - creating a clear, emotionally charged vision of what you're working toward so you always know your 'why'.

2. **Nutrition** - learning how to eat for your goals without restriction, guilt, or confusion.

3. **Training** - learning how to enjoy exercise again with efficient, realistic workouts that give you that toned, athletic look without living in the gym.

4. **Mindset** - developing the mental resilience and identity that keeps it all together, even when life gets hectic and stressful.

5. **Sleep** - improving your recovery, energy, and focus so you can perform better in every area of life.

6. **The Fallback Protocol** - a backup plan for those chaotic weeks that stops you losing control or feeling like you've failed.

7. **Accountability** - the structure that keeps you consistent when motivation fades - because it always will at some point.

Each pillar builds on the last.

You'll start by defining your goals - and why they actually matter to you.

Then you'll learn how to eat and train in a way that's simple, sustainable, and effective.

Next, you'll strengthen your mindset and discover ways to build the essential habits that make progress feel automatic.

And finally, you'll create accountability - the glue that keeps it running smoothly, no matter what life throws at you.

This is the part where it all clicks - where your plan finally works with your life, not against it.

And it all starts with setting the right goals: the kind that actually means something to you.

Get Your **FREE** Fat Loss Toolkit At: **LesterKitching.com/ToolKit**

Build A Powerful Vision

Most people treat goal setting like a box-ticking exercise. They'll say, "I want to lose 10 kilos," or "I want to fit into those jeans again."

But surface-level goals rarely last - because they don't connect to anything *emotional*.

Real transformation starts with clarity and creating a powerful vision. Not just about **what** you want, but **why** you want it.

That's what we will build now.

Start With The Three Year Vision

We're picking a three year timeframe because it's enough time to achieve almost anything you want - if you're willing to put in the work for it.

For most people I work with, three years is a great big-picture timeframe - enough time to get into the best shape of your life while still taking care of your family, performing at work, having fun, and keeping a social life.

Now, imagine your life three years from now.

In three years, you've truly transformed - not just physically, but mentally.

Your health habits are second nature. You train because you want to, not because you "have to."

You're confident, strong, and proud of what you see in the mirror.

You're setting the tone for your family, your colleagues, and the people around you.

Picture that version of you.

How do you look, move, and feel?

What's different in your life because of it?

Who else benefits from this version of you - your kids, your partner, your friends?

That's your **three year vision** - the big picture you're building toward.

Zoom Into The One Year Milestone

Now bring that big vision closer.

If your ultimate transformation is three years away, what would make you proud one year from now?

A year is enough time for a major physical change - even a full lifestyle transformation if you're consistent.

If your goal is smaller, this is where you start solidifying your results and shaping your new identity.

Think about it:

Where do you want to be in 12 months?

What will you have achieved - physically, mentally, emotionally?

What daily actions will the "you a year from now" be doing automatically?

Write that down. That's your **one year goal**.

Focus On The Next 90 Days

Now we bring it into the present. Ninety days is the sweet spot - close enough to stay motivated, long enough to see real results.

If a typical fat loss rate is around **1lb per week**, that's roughly **12lbs (5–6kg)** in 90 days - a realistic target for most people without having to do anything extreme.

If you have more to lose, that number might be higher.

If you're already leaner, it'll likely be less.

But beyond the number, ask yourself:

When does your current situation impact you most?

How does it make you feel right now?

Who else is impacted when you're low on energy, unhappy, or self-conscious?

Then flip it:

How will you feel when you've hit that ninety day goal?

What will improve in your life because of it?

Who else benefits when you're showing up happier, more confident, and full of energy?

That's the emotion you want to attach to your short-term goal - because numbers don't drive action, feelings do.

Common Mistake To Avoid

Setting vague goals or focusing only on numbers.

Most people set goals like "lose weight" or "get fitter," but they never define what that actually means - or why it matters to them. Without a clear picture and emotional connection, goals quickly lose their power, and motivation fades as soon as progress slows.

What To Do Instead

Create a clear, layered vision that connects to emotion.

Start with your three-year vision - the person you want to become and the life you want to live. Zoom into your one-year milestone - what progress looks and feels like. Then lock in your 90-day target - specific, realistic, and emotionally meaningful. This layered approach gives you direction for the long game *and* focus for the short term, so every action has purpose.

Keep Looking At The Map

Setting goals is like choosing a destination - but it's just as important to keep checking the map along the way.

Most people set their goals once and forget them. That's like putting the sat nav on mute 5 minutes after you've set off.

You need regular reminders to stay emotionally connected to what you're working toward.

Those reminders are what pull you through on the days when life gets hard.

So, build a small habit around **reconnecting to your goals**:

You could do this daily, or as part of a weekly review. Even 60 seconds each morning reminding yourself why you started can be powerful and help you stay on track.

You don't need to focus on everything at once. Just pick one thing you're looking forward to (like fitting into those jeans you've not worn for years), or something you're moving away from (that self-conscious feeling when you're standing on the sidelines at your kids' football games).

Your goals aren't static. They'll evolve as you grow and move through the transformation journey - but your *why* and that exciting three year vision will always anchor you.

Measure, But Don't Obsess

Tracking progress is important. It's motivating to see the rewards of your work, and it acts as an alert that we need to fine tune the strategy when progress has stalled.

The most common way to track progress is by stepping on the scale. It's quick and easy, but weight can fluctuate for reasons that have nothing to do with fat loss.

That's why it's smart to track a mix of **metrics**:

Weight: Helps you spot long-term trends, not day-to-day noise. Ideally you track daily, or several times per week and look at your seven day average (most weight tracking apps will do this for you). If you are going to get weighed, the best time is first thing in the morning, after you've been to the toilet and before you've eaten or drank. This approach gives you the best chance of getting a true baseline reading that isn't distorted by daytime variables like food, water, or activity levels.

Measurements: Useful for gauging fat loss even when the scale stalls. Although it can be tricky to measure accurately each time.

Clothes: One of the truest reflections of progress - especially when you train regularly. But it's going to be weeks, not days, before you feel a difference.

Photos: Similar to clothes, they helps you see changes that happen too gradually to notice in real time.

The best solution is using a combination. It balances out the weaknesses of each method and gives you a fuller picture.

Scales give quick, easy, and fast proof of progress - you'll see a change relatively quickly compared to other measures.

But you can counteract the flaws of scales - natural fluctuations that are out of your control and not related to your body fat levels

- by also tracking measurements, the comfort of your clothes, and taking pictures.

Whichever you choose, remember that the real goal isn't to see a certain number on the scales, it's to create a better life.

That could mean playing with your kids at the pool without feeling self-conscious.

Or you feel confident at your Christmas party in that outfit you've been saving.

Or you're waking up with more energy and happiness in your life.

That's what we're really chasing - so while tracking is helpful, it's not something to obsess over.

Focus on your actions and the results will follow.

Common Mistake To Avoid

Letting the scale dictate your emotions and decisions.

Many people get trapped by daily weigh-ins - celebrating every drop, panicking at every spike. But body weight naturally fluctuates due to water, sodium, stress, and hormones. When you tie your self-worth to those numbers, you lose perspective, and motivation quickly crumbles.

What To Do Instead

Track trends, not days - and measure what really matters.

Use a mix of scales, measurements, clothes, and photos to get the full picture. Look at averages and direction over time, not single readings. Most importantly, stay focused on how your life feels - more energy, confidence, and control. The goal isn't just a lighter body; it's a better life.

How Goal Setting Evolves Through The Phases

In the **Ignite phase**, goals give you direction and excitement. You're fired up by the idea of change and for the first time in a long time, the future looks motivating instead of frustrating. Those clear, emotionally-connected goals remind you why you started every time things feel new or uncomfortable.

In the **Momentum phase**, you start ticking off big milestones - and it feels incredible. You see physical changes, people compliment you, and you realise this isn't a dream anymore... it's happening. You may hit your original goal, and replace it with one that's less aligned with weight, clothes sizes or measurements, and more around fitness or energy.

In the **Identity phase**, your goals now become about protecting what you've accomplished and expanding the life you've built. You take pride in maintaining what most people lose. You shift from chasing finish lines to choosing new challenges because growth is now part of who you are. Your goals keep you focused forward - not because you're unhappy, but because you've become someone who expects more from life and believes they can get it.

Get Your **FREE** Fat Loss Toolkit At: <u>LesterKitching.com/ToolKit</u>

Nutrition Simplified

There's a lot of noise around nutrition - macros, meal plans, 'clean eating', fasting, keto, supplements, and everything in between.

But when you strip away the noise, fat loss comes down to one thing:

A calorie deficit.

You have to consistently eat fewer calories than you burn.

Every diet that's ever worked does so because it helps you do that.

So the best diet isn't the one that looks perfect - it's the one you can actually stick to.

The Big Rocks Of Nutrition

There are a few things that make the biggest difference when it comes to both fat loss and how you feel day to day. These are the **big rocks** - the things worth focusing your energy on.

1. Calories - The Foundation

Without a calorie deficit, nothing happens.

That doesn't mean you need to obsess over every gram or live on a tracking app.

It means you need awareness - enough to make adjustments when needed.

A simple way to set your first calorie target:

Body weight (in lbs) × 10–12

(Lower end if you have less activity or a lot of weight to lose. Higher end if you're moderately active.)

That's it.

No complicated math.

This gives you a realistic starting point - then you adjust based on results.

Even the more advanced calculators are only estimates - they can't predict your exact metabolism, stress, movement, sleep, or hormones. So think of your first calorie target as a **starting experiment**, not a final answer.

Here's the key if you want to track calories.

Track daily, weigh daily (first thing in the morning), and watch how the 7-day average moves. You don't have to do this forever, but daily weigh ins give you fast data to make decisions from.

- **If your weight is trending down steadily?** Keep calories where they are.

- **If your weight isn't moving at all?** Lower calories by 100-200 calories.

- **If your weight is dropping too fast?** Increase by 100-200.

Your body will give you the feedback, and you can adjust calories to the right level so you can make progress, without starving yourself.

2. Protein - The Body-Shaper

Protein helps you build and maintain muscle during a fat loss phase.

Aim for roughly **1.8g per kg (0.8g per pound)** of body weight per day as a guide.

If you have a lot of weight to lose, base it on your **goal body weight** instead so you don't have an excessively high protein target.

That'll give you a realistic amount to aim for without forcing excessive amounts of protein-rich foods.

3. Fibre, Vitamins, Minerals, and Water - The Support Team

Fibre helps digestion and fullness.

Vitamins and minerals keep you healthy and energised.

Water keeps everything working properly - aim for 2–3 litres a day.

These aren't 'fat loss hacks' - they're basics that support overall health, and if neglected, can create issues that harm fat loss.

4. Carbs and Fats - The Balance

Don't overcomplicate this. You need both.

Carbs fuel training and recovery.

Fats support hormones and brain function.

The exact ratio doesn't matter - just don't cut out either.

Adjust based on preference and how your body feels, but don't place too much emphasis on the exact amounts.

5. Supplements - The Extras

Supplements are like accessories - they can help, but they're not essential.

A basic supplement bundle that covers most people is:

- Whey protein (for hitting your protein target conveniently if you struggle to do so through what you eat)

- Creatine monohydrate (one of the most research-backed supplements for strength, muscle, and recovery). Any other variations of creatine are going to be more expensive without any significant benefit - monohydrate is all you need.

- Multivitamin (an inexpensive way to top up vitamins and minerals you might miss in your diet)

You can also consider vitamin D and omega-3s - but they're secondary to nailing calories, protein, and consistency.

Everything else is optional - they won't move the needle compared to nailing calories, protein, and consistency.

Common Mistake To Avoid

Getting lost in nutrition "hacks" and ignoring the basics.

Most people spend their energy debating carbs vs fats, chasing supplements, or trying to eat "perfectly clean." But none of that matters if you're not in a consistent calorie deficit. This obsession with micro-details distracts you from the fundamentals that actually create results - awareness of what you're eating, flexibility, and something that you can stick to.

What To Do Instead

Master the big rocks and don't get distracted.

Focus on eating slightly fewer calories than you burn, getting enough protein, and eating plenty of fruit, veg, and whole foods. Stay hydrated, enjoy a balance of carbs and fats, and use supplements only as support - not as a shortcut.

When you focus on these big rocks, it's simpler, you'll feel better, and make great progress without the overwhelm.

Popular Dieting Approaches (And Who They Actually Work For)

There's no single "best" diet - only what's *best for you*.

Every successful diet works because it helps you eat fewer calories than you burn - in a way you can actually live with.

Here's a deeper look at the most common approaches, when they work well, and when they don't.

Calorie Counting

Calorie counting is one of the most accurate and educational tools for understanding what you're eating.

Apps like MyFitnessPal or MacrosFirst can help you build awareness quickly.

When it works:

- You like structure and data.
- You're motivated by clear targets.
- You want to understand your food choices.

When it doesn't:

- You find tracking stressful or obsessive.
- You end up aiming for perfection rather than progress.

How to make it work for you:

Start by tracking for two weeks to learn your baseline.

Use that insight to build portion awareness, then transition to more intuitive eating once you're confident if you want to.

Intermittent Fasting

This isn't magic - it's simply a way to reduce calorie intake by eating in a shorter window, often 8 hours on, 16 off.

When it works:

- You're not hungry in the morning.
- You prefer fewer, larger meals.
- You have a predictable schedule.

When it doesn't:

- You train early in the day and feel sluggish fasted.
- You end up overeating later due to extreme hunger.

How to make it work for you:

Have your first meal later in the day, focus on protein and fibre, and avoid turning your eating window into an all-you-can-eat buffet at night.

Intuitive Eating

The goal for everyone long-term is to eat intuitively - listening to hunger, fullness, and enjoyment cues.

But true intuitive eating takes practice and awareness first.

When it works:

- You've already built strong eating habits.
- You know roughly what your body needs to maintain or lose weight.
- You're tired of tracking but still mindful of choices.

When it doesn't:

- You're new to nutrition awareness.
- You struggle with portion control or use food for comfort - which is normal and can be improved with awareness.

How to make it work for you:

Start by eating slowly, paying attention to fullness, and checking in mid-meal ("Am I still hungry, or just eating because it's there?").

Meal Prep And Structured Plans

Sometimes, simplicity wins. Having set meals prepped in advance removes decision fatigue and helps you stay on track when life gets busy.

When it works:

- You prefer routine.

- You're time-poor and need convenience.
- You want fewer food decisions each day.

When it doesn't:

- You crave flexibility and variety.
- You travel often or eat out regularly.

How to make it work for you:

Batch cook once or twice a week, but allow flexibility for weekends or social occasions.

Which One Is Best For You?

Every one of these methods can work - *if* you can sustain it.

They all share the same principle:

A diet only works if it helps you eat less than you burn - and you can stick to it long enough to see results.

So the best one isn't the one that looks perfect on paper.

It's the one that fits *your* life, *your* preferences, and *your* level of commitment right now.

Common Mistake To Avoid

Blaming yourself when a diet doesn't work - and giving up entirely.

When people try a new diet, they typically give it everything for a few weeks, and when it doesn't deliver results or they simply can't stick to it any longer, they assume they're the problem - that they lack discipline, willpower, or that their body is somehow "broken." Frustrated and disheartened, they give up, regain the weight, and tell themselves they weren't that bothered anyway… even though deep down, they are.

What To Do Instead

Pick the approach that fits your life - and master the fundamentals.

Every diet that works does so because it helps you eat fewer calories than you burn, in a way you can stick to. Choose a method that suits your lifestyle and preferences - one you could see yourself doing six months from now. Focus on consistency over perfection, flexibility over restriction, and long-term learning over short-term results.

Diet Breaks And Reverse Dieting

You don't have to be in a calorie deficit forever.

In fact, planned **diet breaks** can help you stay consistent long-term.

They give your mind and body a breather - letting you enjoy more food, recover better, and return with fresh motivation.

Usually, every 8–12 weeks of dieting, take 1–2 weeks at maintenance calories.

This approach is easier to stick to because you can work hard knowing there's a break coming - rather than staring at an endless timeline. That can be a much easier pill to swallow on days when you might be hungry, tired, or it's just been a tough day.

Once you've reached your goal, the mistake is stopping the habits that got you there. And that often means losing focus with nutrition and as a result, drastically increasing calories and going back into old habits - that's how people regain weight.

Instead, **reverse diet** by slowly adding calories back, around 50–150 per day each week, until you find your maintenance point. Over 3–6 weeks, that might mean 200–600 calories more per day than your diet phase, often without any fat gain.

This helps restore hormones, energy, and training performance while keeping your fat loss results.

Control Your Environment (As Much As Possible)

One of the simplest but most powerful strategies for staying consistent with your nutrition is controlling your environment.

If it's not in the house, it can't tempt you.

It's easier to say no once in the supermarket than to say no ten times a day when you walk past the cupboard.

That's easy when you live alone. But with kids, it's a different story. There'll always be snacks in the house. Chocolate bars, crisps, biscuits… They're part of family life - and that's okay.

So instead of aiming for perfection, aim for **strategic control**:

- **Keep trigger foods out of sight.** Don't leave them on the counter or at the front of the cupboard - make them less visible and less convenient.

- **Have your go-to options visible and ready.** Keep fruit, yoghurt, or protein snacks where you'll see them first. Make the "easy" choice the *better* one.

- **Buy smaller quantities.** A single multi-pack of crisps is easier to manage than a bulk box that's always within reach.

- **Serve in portions, don't snack from the pack.** If you're going to have something, portion it out - avoid eating straight from the bag.

The same principle applies at work - keeping snacks nearby creates a fight you don't need and drains your willpower.

Try this instead:

- Keep water, fruit, or protein snacks in easy reach.

- Don't keep tempting foods in your immediate space - make them something you'd have to go and buy if you really want them.

- Pair that with good pre-planning: if you bring lunch with foods you actually enjoy, you're less likely to wander into the canteen or café and make impulsive choices that lead to overeating.

Controlling your environment isn't about restriction or fearing food - it's about making overeating less likely.

You're not trying to eliminate every temptation - in fact, you could eat a chocolate bar a day and still get fantastic fat loss results as long as you didn't overeat your calories. But having a lot of food that's easy to overeat in your environment just makes it harder than it needs to be.

When you're clear on your goals and emotionally connected to them, the pull of those temptations starts to fade - and the choices that once felt like a battle become almost effortless.

Common Mistake To Avoid

Most people think they just need to be more disciplined around food - to "try harder" next time.

But willpower is limited. After a long day at work, the kids are in bed, and you finally sit down - that's when the biscuits in the cupboard win. It's not a lack of self-control - it's a predictable human response to fatigue and temptation.

What To Do Instead

You don't need to fight cravings all day if you set your environment up to support your goals.

Keep tempting foods out of sight, stock up on better options, and plan your surroundings so that staying on track takes less effort. And remember - once you've built stronger focus and motivation (which we'll cover in the *Mindset* section), those temptations start to lose their grip.

Your 3×3 For Simple And Enjoyable Nutrition

One of the easiest ways to simplify your nutrition is to create your own **3×3**.

That means having **three go-to options for each of your three main meals** (breakfast, lunch, and dinner) - that you genuinely enjoy and can repeat without boredom.

These are your 'no-brainer' meals for busy days or low motivation.

They remove decision fatigue, reduce the urge to grab something random, and keep you consistent even when life gets hectic.

You don't need gourmet recipes or endless variety.

These will most likely be relatively quick and easy to prepare, but still enjoyable to eat. You just need reliable meals that tick the boxes for **protein, produce, and portion control.**

Here's what it might look like in practice:

Breakfast: (1) Greek yoghurt bowl, (2) overnight oats, (3) omelette with veggies

Lunch: (1) Chicken salad, (2) wrap with lean protein and veggies, (3) protein yoghurt, nuts and berries.

Dinner: (1) Stir-fry, (2) grilled meat or fish with veg, (3) chilli or curry bowl

That's your 3×3 - simple, quick, effective. No calorie counting, spreadsheets, or stress required.

There are no special recipes. Just aim to finish each day hitting the main rocks - calories, protein, fibre, water, and a roughly even split of carbs and fats.

Common Mistake To Avoid

Overcomplicating your nutrition and trying to build a brand-new menu every week.

Most people assume variety is the key to success, but too much choice leads to decision fatigue - and that's when the quick, easy, less-helpful options start creeping in.

What To Do Instead

Keep things simple and repeatable.

Build a short list of go-to meals you enjoy and can prepare quickly - your personal 3×3. That structure gives you freedom, not restriction. When life gets busy, you'll always have options that keep you on track without thinking too hard.

Guilt-Free Socialising

Fat loss doesn't mean giving up your social life. In fact, if your plan doesn't allow you to eat out, enjoy drinks, or have your favourite food every now and then - it's not a plan you'll stick to. The goal isn't perfection - it's balance. You want to be able to enjoy meals with friends, family nights in, or drinks at the weekend without guilt, restriction, or undoing your progress.

Here's how to make it work:

Make Smart Swaps

You don't have to cut everything out - just make smart choices.

Choose Coke Zero instead of Coke. Go for a light beer instead of pints. Pick a gin with slimline tonic over sugary mixers. These small swaps easily save hundreds of calories without feeling like you're missing out.

Don't Go Overboard

You can absolutely enjoy a takeaway or a meal out - just stop when you're satisfied, not stuffed.

Eat slowly, enjoy the food, and move on.

Balance beats guilt every time.

Bank Calories For Flexibility

You don't have to eat the same number of calories every day. Think weekly, not daily - it's the key to flexibility without guilt.

If you've got a night out or a meal planned, you can "bank" calories by eating a little lighter during the week. For example, trimming 200 calories Monday to Friday gives you 1,000 extra to enjoy at the weekend - without going off track.

Go No Or Low with Alcohol

Alcohol can be a progress killer, and if you're looking for better health, as well as fat loss, going no or low alcohol is recommended. If you want to drink, know that it comes with trade-offs: empty calories, disrupted sleep, and poor food choices the next day.

If you drink, do it mindfully. Stick to lower-calorie options, have water between drinks, and understand that every decision has a cost - but that doesn't mean you can't enjoy yourself.

Enjoy It, Then Move On

Guilt serves no purpose here.

You don't need to "make up" for a meal out or punish yourself in the gym the next day.

Just get straight back to your normal routine. That's what balance looks like - and that's what makes this approach sustainable for life.

Because if you can enjoy the social side of life while still moving toward your goals, you've cracked one of the hardest parts of transformation.

Common Mistake To Avoid

Trying to be "all or nothing" when it comes to socialising.

Many people go through cycles of being ultra-strict during the week, then completely letting go at the weekend - only to feel guilty and start over on Monday. This on-off approach creates a frustrating loop where progress constantly resets, and food becomes something you either "earn" or "make up for."

What To Do Instead

Plan, enjoy, and move on.

See social occasions as part of your plan, not a break from it. Make small swaps, bank calories, enjoy yourself, and get straight back to your normal routine the next day - no guilt, no punishment, just balance.

The goal isn't to avoid real life - it's to live it fully while still making progress. When you master that, you've built a lifestyle you can keep forever.

Recognising And Managing Overeating Patterns

Overeating isn't about willpower - it's about patterns that make it easier to eat more than you need or even want.

Most people don't even realise *why* they're overeating until after it's happened. But when you understand the trigger behind it, you can plan around it and break the cycle without guilt or shame.

Here are the most common overeating triggers - and how to handle each one.

Boredom Eating

When life feels repetitive, food becomes entertainment. You're not hungry - you're just searching for something to fill the gap. The act of eating gives you a little dopamine hit, and for a few minutes, it feels like you're doing something productive. The problem is, that short-term relief often turns into long-term frustration.

This can be very common with parents of older children. When they are younger, they are dependent on you and it's like you don't have time to be bored. As children grow up and become more independent, parents now have more free time than they used to and boredom eating can set in - typically on an evening when the kids are playing with friends, at after-school clubs, or playing video games on their own.

How to handle it:

- Create a "bored list" - five quick things you can do instead of eating that you enjoy.

- Keep snacks out of sight as we covered in the *Controlling Your Environment* section early - it's far easier to say no once in the supermarket than ten times a day at home.

- Before reaching for food, pause and ask: "Am I actually hungry, or just looking for something to do?"

Stress Or Low-Mood Eating

When you're stressed, food can act as comfort. The process of eating - especially sweet, salty, or high-fat foods - gives a temporary emotional release. But it's like putting a plaster on a deeper issue: the stress or sadness is still there when the food's gone, and you often feel worse after.

Over time, this link between food and emotion becomes a habit loop that reinforces each time it occurs.

How to handle it:

- Identify your stress triggers - work overload, arguments, lack of sleep, or feeling undervalued.
- Use non-food stress relievers - deep breathing, journaling, walking, or calling someone supportive.
- If you do eat, do it mindfully - sit down, eat slowly, and actually taste the food. It turns the experience from a coping mechanism into a conscious choice.

Social Eating

Food brings people together - and that's a good thing. But social events can quickly become calorie landmines when "special occasions" start happening every weekend. It can even be at-home rituals like Friday night takeaway or a big Sunday dinner with the family.

It's easy to fall into the mindset of 'I'll just start again Monday,' which often leads to guilt and inconsistency.

How to handle it:

- Plan ahead - have a balanced meal before you go out so you're not starving when food arrives. And adjust your eating the days before to account for a higher calorie event.

- Decide your non-negotiables - maybe it's enjoying drinks but skipping dessert, or sharing starters instead of ordering your own.

- Focus on connection, not consumption - enjoy the conversation and the company instead of treating the night like an eating competition.

Mindless Eating

This happens when you eat without thinking - in front of the TV, scrolling your phone, or snacking straight from the packet. You're disconnected from what you're eating, so your brain doesn't register fullness until you're already over it.

It's one of the most common overeating patterns because it's automatic and rarely noticed in the moment.

How to handle it:

- Eat without distractions - even turning off the TV or putting your phone down can make a huge difference.

- Portion your food before sitting down - don't eat straight from the bag or container.

- When you're done, leave the kitchen or lounge area - staying nearby makes it easier to "pick" at food out of habit.

Fast Eating

Another hidden overeating pattern is eating too quickly. When you eat fast, you don't give yourself enough time to register fullness, so you often end up eating far more than you need before your brain catches up.

If you've ever watched eating challenges on YouTube or social media, you've seen this principle in action - those competitors eat incredibly fast because it allows them to get more food in before they feel full.

For fat loss, that principle works in reverse. The slower you eat, the more time your body has to recognise fullness. You'll naturally stop earlier, feel satisfied, and consume fewer calories - all without changing what's on your plate.

How to handle it:

- Slow down - put your fork down between bites, take a sip of water, or simply pause after each mouthful.

- Pay attention to the taste and texture of your food. Enjoy it rather than rushing through it.

- If you tend to eat distracted (in front of the TV or scrolling), remove the distractions and be more present with your meal.

You don't need to overthink it - just slow down enough to notice when you've had enough.

Reward Eating

You've had a long day, hit your workout, or finished a stressful week - so you "deserve" something. That logic feels harmless, but when every win is rewarded with food or drink, progress slows and your brain starts linking success with overeating.

It becomes a subtle, well-meaning trap that ultimately can slow, then derail your fat loss progress.

How to handle it:

- Celebrate with something that *reinforces* your progress - a day trip to somewhere new, a new book, a hot bath, or new gym gear.

- Still want food? That's fine - just make it intentional, not automatic. Sit down, enjoy it, and don't go overboard. Keep your long term vision in mind.

- Remember: the real reward is how you *feel* after a good day, not just what you eat because of it.

Common Mistake To Avoid

Blaming yourself for overeating - instead of understanding it.

Most people see overeating as a lack of discipline, when it's actually a predictable response to boredom, stress, emotion, or environment. That guilt keeps the cycle alive and makes it harder to change long term.

What To Do Instead

Get curious, not critical.

When you notice yourself overeating, pause and ask, "What's really happening here?" The moment you can name the pattern, you can plan for it. And once you plan for it, you're no longer stuck in the same loop - you're in control of it.

Managing Hunger

Feeling hungry doesn't mean you're doing anything wrong. It's completely normal, and it's often a sign that your calories are at a good level for fat loss.

We just want to be mindful of how hungry we are - if it's occasional and noticeable but not too extreme, that's not an issue.

It becomes a problem when you're *very* hungry, feeling light-headed, unwell, or unable to concentrate.

If you've been cutting calories too long, you might also struggle to keep your portions in check when you do eat, or find yourself craving 'junk' food all the time.

That's not the type of hunger we're aiming for (but it might feel familiar if you've done crash diets in the past).

The key is to know how to manage hunger so it doesn't control you.

Here are six steps or mindset shifts to keep hunger low enough that you can still feel great while losing fat:

Use The 20-Minute Rule

When hunger hits, don't rush to eat. Drink 500ml of water, then do something to occupy your mind for 20 minutes. Go for a walk, message a friend, tidy something up.

Most of the time, that wave of hunger will pass, and you'll start to realise how much of your "hunger" was just habit, not actual need.

Bulk Out Your Meals

If you're naturally someone who feels hunger more intensely, volume eating will be your best friend. Add more veggies or salads to your meals which are low in calories but take up space, keeping you fuller for longer.

A big portion of vegetables might add 50 calories, but it could stop you reaching for 300–500 calories' worth of snacks later. That's a smart trade-off every time.

Know The Difference Between Hunger And Boredom

Sometimes it's not hunger - it's habit or boredom. Here's a simple test: would you eat a nice, but rather unexciting meal; let's say a baked potato with chicken breast and salad?

If yes, you're probably hungry. If not, it's likely you're just bored.

Fix the boredom - not with food, but by doing something that engages you. You'll feel better for it, and you'll build awareness of what's really going on.

Keep The Big Goal In Mind

When you're hungry, zoom out. Remind yourself what you're working toward - more confidence, energy, and control.

If it's mild hunger, and you aren't feeling unwell, it's not something to fear.

Each time you handle it calmly, you're strengthening your resilience and proving to yourself that you're in control.

Use Diet Breaks To Recharge

A smart strategy includes diet breaks. Every 8–12 weeks, spend 1–2 weeks on maintenance calories. You'll feel more energised, hunger will drop, and mentally, it becomes easier knowing you're not hungry forever, just until your next planned break.

Maintenance Isn't A Diet

Once you've reached your goal, you don't need to stay in a deficit forever.

You can (and should) increase calories to maintenance - meaning you can eat more while keeping your results.

Understanding that this isn't forever can really help you push through hunger pangs when you'd normally feel overwhelmed and quit the plan.

Common Mistake To Avoid

Treating hunger as a problem to fix.

Most people panic when hunger shows up, assuming they've done something wrong or that they can't handle it. They eat impulsively and break their plan, then feel frustrated and lose trust in themselves.

What To Do Instead

Expect hunger, plan for it, and use the tools above to manage it.

It's not about avoiding hunger - it's about understanding it and implementing the right actions or mindset shifts. When you can stay calm and mindful through those moments, you stay in control, and that's when real progress happens.

Once you can manage hunger with confidence, nutrition stops feeling like a battle - and starts feeling like freedom.

How Nutrition Evolves Through the Phases

In the **Ignite phase**, your focus is awareness - learning what's really in your food and starting to create structure. You might track calories, and build a handful of simple go-to meals.

In **Momentum**, things feel smoother. You've got routines that work, and you start making tweaks based on your goals - adjusting calories, trying new recipes to avoid boredom, or taking diet breaks when you're feeling a little burnt out.

By the **Identity phase**, eating well is automatic. You're not 'on a plan' anymore - you've built a way of eating that fits your life, your preferences, and your goals. It's not effort - it's who you are now. You may track calories for short bursts if you feel like you're slipping and you want to put a spotlight on your eating habits.

Bringing It Together

Nutrition doesn't have to be complicated. It just has to be consistent.

When you focus on the big rocks - calories, protein, fibre, balance, and habits - you build a structure that lasts.

You stop bouncing between extremes, stop feeling guilty around food, and finally start to feel in control.

Get this right, and fat loss becomes inevitable.

In the next section, we'll build on this foundation and look at how to **train effectively around real life** - without long workouts, fancy equipment, or burnout.

Get Your **FREE** Fat Loss Toolkit At: **LesterKitching.com/ToolKit**

Get Your **FREE** Fat Loss Toolkit At: LesterKitching.com/ToolKit

Training That Fits Real Life

Most people think they need endless hours in the gym to see real results - they don't.

You can make visible, lasting changes to your body and confidence with just two to four focused sessions per week - if you train the right way and back it up with good nutrition.

During fat loss, the goal of training isn't to burn as many calories as possible - it's to build and keep muscle while you lose fat. That's what gives your body the shape and tone you want.

When people say they want to 'tone up', what they really mean is revealing lean muscle under reduced body fat.

That's what training is for.

It's not punishment for eating, or a chore you have to survive.

It's the thing that helps you shape your body, feel stronger, move better, and stay mentally sharp.

How Often You Need To Train (And How To Make It Efficient When You're Short On Time)

You don't need to live in the gym.

Two to four focused sessions a week is plenty - especially when life's busy and time's short.

Here's a simple guide to help you plan:

- **2 days per week:** full body both days.

- **3 days per week:** full body or upper/lower split.

- **4 days per week:** upper/lower or push/pull/legs.

If life gets in the way, shift things around. Drop to two sessions if you're stretched, or bump to four if you've got the time and energy.

If you're short on time, one of the smartest ways to train is with **antagonistic supersets** - pairing opposite muscle groups so you can get more done in less time.

Think of it like alternating between push and pull exercises: you train one muscle group while the other rests.

For example:

- Bench Press then Barbell Row

- Shoulder Press then Pull-Ups

- Squats then Hamstring Curls

This method keeps your heart rate up, saves rest time, and makes workouts feel faster and more engaging.

It's also ideal for full-body sessions where you need to fit a lot into a short window.

If you prefer keeping exercises separate, or you can't easily do supersets in your gym, that's fine too - but supersets are a great option when life's busy, or when you just want to be in and out in under 45 minutes.

Common Mistake To Avoid

Thinking you need to train every day or for hours to see results.

Most people overcommit - training five or six times a week until life inevitably gets in the way - then give up entirely when they can't stick to that 'perfect' plan. The result? Burnout, inconsistency, and constant restarts. Short workouts aren't the problem - unsustainable ones are.

What To Do Instead

Train with focus and efficiency, not duration.

Two to four purposeful sessions per week is more than enough to build muscle, lose fat, and feel strong - especially when using time-efficient methods like supersets. Pair opposing muscle groups, keep rest purposeful, and stay consistent. Progress isn't about doing more - it's about doing enough, consistently, in a way that fits your life.

Volume, Progression, And Recovery

You don't need a crazy amount of volume to see results.

Everyone is different in how responsive their body is to training, but typically **6-10 per muscle group per week** is the sweet spot for most people. That's enough to build or maintain muscle during a fat loss phase - especially when combined with solid nutrition.

Any more than that offers diminishing returns, and for busy people, the extra time in the gym usually isn't worth the trade-off.

If you're only able, or willing to train twice a week, you can still make great progress as long as you are maximising your time in the gym.

But what matters more than volume is **progression**.

Your body only changes when you give it a reason to.

That means doing a little more over time - not every session, but across the weeks and months ahead.

Here's what progression typically looks like:

- Lifting a slightly heavier weight for the same reps.
- Doing an extra rep or two with the same weight.

These are the most common, easy-to-track signs of overload, and ensure that you are stimulating your muscle.

For big compound lifts (squats, deadlifts, presses), rest 1–3 minutes between sets. For smaller movements (curls, lateral raises, crunches), rest 30–90 seconds.

If you're training hard, don't rush rest. Recovery between sets lets you train with intensity and actually progress.

For simplicity, rather than watching the clock, go again once you've caught your breath.

Common Mistake To Avoid

Trying to do too much and burning out.

A lot of people start motivated and load up their training - long sessions, high volume, and barely any rest - forgetting they also have jobs, families, and everyday responsibilities. After a few weeks, they're exhausted, stressed, and struggling to keep up. Eventually, training becomes another source of pressure instead of progress, and consistency falls apart.

What To Do Instead

Find the minimum effective dose and build from there.

Do enough to make progress, not as much as possible. Ten hard sets per muscle group each week is plenty when paired with solid nutrition and recovery. Train with purpose, rest well between sets, and focus on small, steady improvements. This balanced approach helps you stay consistent for months - not just a few frantic weeks before life catches up.

Exercise Selection, Rep Ranges And How Hard To Train

Most of your training should revolve around **compound movements** - exercises that work multiple muscles at once.

They give you the biggest return for your effort.

These include:

- Squats and lunges
- Deadlifts and hip hinges
- Presses (bench, overhead, dumbbell)
- Rows and pulldowns
- Carries and planks

Mix in **unilateral work** like split squats or single-arm rows for variety, or to replace bigger lifts when you need a change.

A good general guide for rep ranges is 5–20 per set.

Any lower, and you're focusing much more on strength than building/retaining muscle. Any higher, and you're working more into endurance.

Ideally, work through a variety of rep ranges - either within a single session or across the week.

For example, you might train Monday and Thursday, squatting on both days.

On Monday, you train 5–10 reps; on Thursday, 15–20 reps.

An alternative would be to do one set at 5-10 reps, another at 10-15 reps, and the final set at 15-20 reps on both Monday and Thursday.

Results will be virtually the same, so choose based on preference.

The key is to train **close to failure** - ideally stopping when you've got one or two good reps left in the tank.

If you finish a set and feel like you could've done five more, it's likely too far from failure to maximise results.

Beginners can push closer to failure safely because the weights are lighter and fatigue-related injury risk is lower. It's much easier to train close to failure, squatting 50kg as a beginner, than 150kg as an advanced lifter.

Technique also plays an important role in your training. The best results and lower injury risk will be seen with control, moving through the full range of motion.

Ideally, your reps look identical until the last few, where technique may fade slightly and rep speed slows.

It's not about throwing weights around - it's about controlling them.

Common Mistake To Avoid

Chasing variety or volume instead of mastery.

A lot of people constantly change exercises, or copy advanced routines they see online - thinking more variety or more work equals better results. In reality, this constant switching prevents you from ever getting strong or skilled enough at the basics to make real progress.

Others go the opposite way - doing endless easy reps that never get close enough to failure to actually stimulate muscle growth.

What To Do Instead

Master the fundamentals and train with intent.

Build your training around the big compound lifts and aim to get stronger at them over time. Use a mix of rep ranges, but make sure every set challenges you - finishing with just one or two solid reps left in the tank.

Keep your form tight, your control deliberate, and your effort consistent. Real progress doesn't come from novelty - it comes from doing the simple things with precision and purpose.

Cardio, Conditioning, And Movement

Strength training already improves your cardio health - especially if you use supersets or keep rest periods short.

But adding extra cardio can help your fitness and support fat loss if you've got the time in your schedule to do it.

If fat loss is the goal, choose an extra weights session over an extra cardio session.

However, if cardio is very important to you - you love it, or you're setting a fitness goal such as a half marathon - incorporate it into your training plan.

Beyond workouts, moving more in daily life helps your fat loss goal. Taking the stairs, going for a walk at lunch, playing a sport, can all mean you're burning more calories while improving your overall health.

Deload Weeks - When to Pull Back

If you've been training consistently for a while, it's normal to build up a bit of fatigue.

That doesn't just mean feeling tired - it can show up as stiffness, aches, low motivation, or workouts that just don't feel the same.

For most people training 2–4 days per week, especially if you're not pushing very heavy weights, you don't need to schedule deloads too often. But it's still worth knowing the signs that your body (and mind) could use a short break.

Here are a few signs you might need to ease off for a week:

- Your strength has stalled or dropped for more than a couple of sessions in a row.

- You feel unusually sore, stiff, or achy - even from lighter workouts.

- You dread going to the gym or find it hard to get motivated.

- You're not sleeping well or feeling run down.

- Your joints or tendons feel irritated rather than just 'worked'.

If that sounds like you, take what's called a **deload week**.

This doesn't mean seven days on the sofa - it means pulling back intentionally.

Go to the gym but drop loads to 50% of normal and halve your sets or total time.

You could even swap the gym for a walk or swim that week - or rest completely, as long as daily movement stays up.

A week like this gives your muscles, joints, and nervous system time to recover and come back stronger. You'll often feel hungrier to train again - and that's exactly what we want.

Remember: a week of easier training doesn't derail progress - it protects it.

As long as your nutrition and sleep stay on track, you'll return feeling better,stronger, and making faster progress than if you tried to grind through exhaustion.

Common Mistake To Avoid

Pushing through fatigue because you're afraid of losing progress.

For people who are overtraining, they ignore the signs that their body needs a break - sore joints, poor sleep, stalled lifts, or low motivation - and keep pushing harder out of guilt or fear of going backwards. But this usually leads to burnout, nagging injuries, or even regression, because your body never gets the chance to fully recover.

What To Do Instead

Pull back to move forward.

A deload week isn't a failure - it's a strategy. When you reduce volume and intensity for a short period, your body repairs, your energy returns, and your motivation resets. You come back stronger, not softer. Think of deloads as part of progress, not a pause from it - a smart way to keep making gains long after everyone else has burnt out.

The Real-World Reframe

There's no perfect training plan - just one that fits your life, challenges you, and keeps you coming back.

If you're training consistently, progressing gradually, and enjoying it, that's what matters.

You don't need a new plan every few weeks. You just need to show up, train hard, and make small, steady improvements over time. That's what creates lasting results.

As your life changes, your training will too - that's normal. You might do less one season, more the next.

The key is that you keep training.

Every time you show up - even for a short session - you're keeping a promise to yourself.

That's how you stay consistent in the real world.

And if you miss a session, you adjust - not restart.

Think about the perfection trap: you aim for three sessions, but life happens.

You get ill. Work runs late. The kids need extra lifts to practice.

With a rigid plan, you fail when you only manage 2 out of 3 workouts, and for someone who's likely struggled with a history of failed attempts to transform their body, every time you go 'off plan', the hit to motivation and confidence is massive.

That's why the Transformation System is set up the way it is - to account for great weeks, but also for the bad ones.

That's how you break the all-or-nothing cycle that keeps most people stuck.

Common Mistake To Avoid

Treating your plan like it only works when life is perfect.

Many people start strong, but the moment something unexpected happens - a busy week at work, a cold, the kids' schedules - they assume they've "failed" and fall completely off track. This rigid, all-or-nothing mindset turns minor detours into full-blown setbacks and keeps you stuck in the cycle of starting over again and again.

What To Do Instead

Adapt instead of abandon.

Real progress comes from flexibility, not perfection. Some weeks you'll train three times, others it might be once - and that's okay. The key is showing up in whatever way you can, keeping the promise you made to yourself, and adjusting instead of restarting.

That's how you stay consistent in the real world - and why this time, your results actually last.

How Training Evolves Through The Phases

In the **Ignite phase**, training is about building the habit - you're learning new exercises, getting used to training at the right effort levels, and maybe adapting to a new gym environment. But in the early days, you should notice quick improvements in your confidence, strength, and fitness.

In **Momentum**, your confidence is growing and you can start chasing progression - adding a little more weight or another rep each session.

By the **Identity phase**, training isn't something you "have to do." It's something you do automatically - part of your lifestyle, and a cornerstone of how you stay strong, capable, and in control.

Bringing It Together

You've now got the physical part of the Transformation System - how to train efficiently, build strength, and stay consistent around real life.

But training is only one piece of the puzzle.

You can have the perfect plan on paper - sets, reps, progression - but if your head's not in the right place, it won't stick.

That's why the next part of the System focuses on your *mindset* - the glue that holds everything together.

Training builds your body.

Mindset builds the person who keeps showing up.

When your physical actions and your mental habits align, you stop forcing progress and start living it.

Because at that point, training isn't something you *have* to do - it's something you *get* to do.

Up next, we'll shift from 'trying to get fit' to becoming a fit person - how to stay motivated, stay resilient, and actually enjoy the process.

Get Your **FREE** Fat Loss Toolkit At: LesterKitching.com/ToolKit

Unstoppable Mindset

Each pillar of the Transformation System builds on the last.

Goal Setting gives us clarity over what we *really* want.

Nutrition creates fat loss.

Training shapes your body for that toned, athletic look.

Now we come to Mindset - the glue that turns short-term progress into long-term change.

Most people don't fail because they're not trying hard enough.

They fail because they still see themselves as someone trying to get fit - not someone who already is.

They follow a plan, maybe even hit a goal, but drift back to square one because the identity never changed.

The real goal isn't to 'do fitness'; it's to be a fit person.

Someone who eats well, moves regularly, and takes care of themselves - not because they have to, but because it's just who they are now.

That's the identity shift - the moment you stop trying to get fit and start living like someone who already is.

You're not 'on a diet'. You're someone who eats with awareness.

You're not 'forcing yourself to work out'. You're someone who trains because it makes you feel good.

You're not 'trying to be disciplined'. You've built a life that supports the habits you want to keep.

Here's the mindset to carry:

- You don't have to be perfect. You just have to stay in the game.

- Progress beats motivation - action builds belief and kills self-doubt.

- Structure > willpower. If it's built into your week, it's far more likely to happen.

- Hold ground on tough weeks. Not sliding backwards is still a win.

Habit Stacking: Make Fat Loss Way Easier

The easiest way to make good habits stick is to design your environment for them. Motivation is finite - and it won't always be there when you need it.

So set yourself up for success by removing friction from the actions that drive results.

Habit stacking, a concept in *James Clear's Atomic Habits*, means connecting new habits to existing ones.

"After I finish work, I go straight to the gym."

"After I make my morning coffee, I fill my water bottle."

"After I put the kids to bed, I prep tomorrow's lunch."

These links make the actions easier because they ride on top of routines you already have.

Next, reduce friction - remove the little barriers that slow you down:

Pack your gym bag the night before rather than doing it during the morning rush.

Keep a healthy snack within reach rather than going to the shop on your lunch break.

Move tempting foods out of sight rather than keeping hyper-palatable 'easy to overeat' foods front and centre.

These might seem small, but they add up. The less effort it takes to make the right choice, the more consistent you'll be.

Small tweaks, big pay-off.

Common Mistake To Avoid

Relying on motivation instead of systems.

Most people assume that if they just *try harder*, they'll finally stay consistent. But motivation is unreliable - it fades when you're tired, stressed, or busy. Without a plan that makes good choices easy and bad choices harder, you'll always feel like you're swimming upstream.

What To Do Instead

Design your environment so the right choice becomes the easy choice.

Use habit stacking to anchor new routines onto things you already do automatically. Reduce friction wherever you can - pack your bag the night before, keep healthy snacks nearby, and move temptation out of sight. You don't need more willpower; you need better systems that make success almost automatic.

The HEAL Principle And Positive Focus

Our brains are wired to spot danger - not progress. That's why it's easy to dismiss wins and magnify mistakes.

Rick Hanson's *Hardwiring Happiness* shares a method called **HEAL** that helps you retrain your focus to look for the positive, and away from the negativity bias that we instinctively possess.

Here's how it works:

- **Have** a positive experience (a win, a good choice, a kind word).

- **Enrich** it - notice it fully, enjoy it for a few seconds.

- **Absorb** it - let that feeling land, so your brain remembers.

- **Link** it (optional) - connect it to a negative moment to help rewire your response.

Example 1 - Nutrition:

You finish dinner feeling comfortably satisfied - not stuffed. Instead of rushing past it, pause and notice that feeling of control and lightness.

That's Enrich.

Take a deep breath and let it sink in - Absorb.

Now, Link it back to the last time you overate and felt sluggish or guilty. You're teaching your brain that this new pattern - eating just enough - feels better.

Example 2 - Training:

You didn't want to train, but you showed up anyway. You leave feeling more energised and proud that you followed through.

Don't just tick it off - stop for a moment to Enrich that win.

Absorb how your body feels stronger, your mind clearer.

Then Link it to the memory of skipping a session and regretting it later. Over time, your brain starts associating showing up with satisfaction instead of effort.

This isn't fluffy thinking - it's mental conditioning. It's easy to get dragged into social media drama and the doom and gloom of the news.

But these negative influences can make us sensitive to minor setbacks, and make us numb to the small wins you're making daily.

When you start recognising wins instead of chasing perfection, you build self-belief and momentum.

End your day with three simple questions:

1. What wins did I have today?

2. What challenged me?

3. What did I learn or handle better than before?

If this is new, some days will be easier than others. Some days you'll feel on top of the world. Others you might not feel like you've had any wins at all.

But over time, you'll build a long list of wins - reminders that you are making progress, even on the tough days.

These reflections can shift your mindset faster than any motivational quote. They come from your own experiences, and specifically for your circumstances.

Common Mistake To Avoid

Overlooking your wins and obsessing over what went wrong.

Most people are quick to criticise themselves but slow to acknowledge progress. Over time, that trains your brain to expect failure - even when you're improving. This constant self-criticism kills motivation, lowers confidence, and makes it harder to stay consistent when life gets tough.

What To Do Instead

Actively train your brain to notice progress.

Use the HEAL principle to turn small wins into lasting confidence. When something goes well, pause for a few seconds - enrich it, absorb it, and let it sink in. Link it to a time you struggled, and notice how far you've come.

The more you practice this, the more naturally your mind will focus on progress instead of problems - and that shift changes everything about how you feel, act, and stay consistent.

The Real-Life Reset

Bad weeks are inevitable - what matters is how you respond.

Use this simple 3-step reset to get back on track quickly:

1. **Review** - What went off track? Be honest, not harsh. This isn't about blame; it's about clarity so you can minimise the impact.

2. **Refocus** - What's one thing you can do today to make progress or hold ground? This shifts you into a proactive mindset and ownership of next steps. You might not always be able to control the situation - the car broke down so you couldn't get to the gym - but you can control what you choose to do next.

3. **Rebuild** - Pick up tomorrow like nothing happened. Learn from the experience if possible so it doesn't come up again in future, and move on. What's done is done. There's no benefit to punishing yourself.

Do this and you'll recover from setbacks faster. Your bounce-back speed is one of the best signs of progress..

Common Mistake To Avoid

Letting one bad day turn into a bad week.

Most people see a setback as failure - missing a workout, overeating, or having a stressful week - and then spiral into "what's the point?" thinking. That all-or-nothing mindset leads to guilt, inconsistency, and starting over again and again.

What To Do Instead

Focus on how fast you can reset, not how perfectly you can perform.

Use the simple 3-step reset - Review, Refocus, Rebuild - to get back on track quickly. Reflect honestly without blame, take one positive action today, and move on tomorrow like nothing happened. The goal isn't to avoid every setback; it's to shorten the gap between falling off and getting back up. That's real progress.

Refine, Don't Restart

Once you've reached your ultimate goal, resist the urge to think 'I've made it, I don't need to do these things anymore'.

If your structure helped you lose fat, a simplified version of that same structure will help you maintain it.

It takes far less effort to maintain results than to earn them - but be mindful of how much you change.

You might shorten your workouts but keep the same days, or drop one session while keeping the same structure.

Or you might stop tracking calories but still follow the core principles and eating pattern.

This isn't you starting over - you're evolving.

Common Mistake To Avoid

Stopping the things that got you there.

After reaching their goal, many people relax a little too much - skipping workouts, dropping nutrition habits, or losing the structure that made success possible. Without those foundations, old patterns slowly return, and progress starts to slip away before they realise it.

What To Do Instead

Refine, don't restart.

Once you've achieved your goal, make small, intentional adjustments rather than a total reset. Train a bit less, loosen tracking, or ease your routine - but keep the core habits that built your success. You're not starting over; you're transitioning from transformation to maintenance, where the goal is control and enjoying the life you've worked hard to create.

Zoom Out When You Start To Drift

It's normal to have quieter phases where you lose a bit of sharpness. You might have a period of time where your life commitments shift, for better or worse, and you end up slipping back.

The key is to recognise it early and tighten things back up.

A common problem here is getting disheartened and throwing it all away.

Instead, zoom out and see the bigger picture.

Over a year, there'll naturally be peaks, plateaus, and dips. What matters is the overall trend.

If your goal is a particular weight, you aren't going to hit it and then stay at that exact point forever.

A strategy that works well is to live within an acceptable range.

So rather than expecting to stay at 140 lbs forever, give yourself a range - say 135 to 145. This accounts for natural ups and downs, but the top and bottom of the range act as a warning siren that you're getting too relaxed with exercise and nutrition, and you need to refocus for a few weeks..

When you catch yourself slipping, don't panic - go back to the basics that built your success:

- Solid sleep
- Simple nutrition
- Consistent movement
- Accountability

You don't need something new or extreme. You just need to reconnect with what's already worked for you.

Common Mistake To Avoid

Panicking when progress slows or slips.

When people notice themselves drifting or the number on the scales go up one day, they often see it as failure and overreact - either giving up completely or swinging to unsustainable extremes to "fix" it. This all-or-nothing mindset turns a small setback into a full reset.

What To Do Instead

Zoom out and look at the bigger picture.

Progress isn't linear - it ebbs and flows. Instead of chasing perfection, give yourself a healthy range to live within and treat small slips as signals, not setbacks. When things drift, go back to your proven basics: sleep well, eat simply, move consistently, and stay accountable. That's what brings you back on track - without the chaos.

Shift From Outcome To Identity - And Stay Future Focused

At the start of your transformation, everything's about what you want to achieve:

Lose fat and get that toned, athletic look.

Build confidence.

Finally feel in control.

Those goals give you direction and motivation - they pull you forward when things feel hard. But once you've achieved them, your focus has to evolve. You're no longer chasing results - you're protecting what you've built. That's a new phase - and one most people overlook.

When the initial excitement fades, it's easy to drift. You might start relaxing on nutrition, skipping workouts, or thinking "I'll get back on it next week." It happens quietly - not because you've failed, but because you've reached the point where discipline must be replaced by identity.

The real goal now is to become the kind of person who *naturally* maintains their progress.

You're not "trying to lose weight."

You're a person who exercises regularly, eats well most of the time, manages stress, and keeps balance in your life.

You're no longer defined by chasing the next milestone - you're living the habits that once felt hard until they became second nature.

And that's what separates short-term success from long-term transformation.

But that doesn't mean your journey ends here.

Your transformation doesn't stop when you reach your goal weight - it just changes shape.

Once you've reached your original target, maintaining it can sometimes feel like a boring goal, so it helps to set new challenges that keep you motivated and growing.

That could mean:

- Training for a 10K.
- Learning a new skill or type of training at the gym.
- Hitting a strength milestone.
- Feeling confident by the pool on holiday.

Future goals give your training and nutrition purpose beyond the scale.

They keep you progressing and living the habits that got you here - not because you have to, but because you *want* to.

When actions align with identity, consistency doesn't need to be forced - it just happens.

Common Mistake To Avoid

Stopping once you reach your goal.

Many people hit their target weight or fitness goal and think the job's done. They ease off their training, relax their nutrition, and slowly drift back into old habits - not out of laziness, but because they never shifted their mindset from "achieving" to "maintaining." Without a new sense of purpose, it's easy to lose momentum, feel unmotivated, and gradually undo months of progress.

What To Do Instead

Shift from chasing results to living the lifestyle.

Keep doing the simple habits that got you there - training, eating well, managing stress - but without the pressure of perfection. Then, set fresh goals that excite you and keep you moving forward. You're not finishing a plan; you're living a new normal.

How Mindset Evolves Through The Phases

In the **Ignite phase**, mindset work is intentional. You're learning to spot wins, break the "all-or-nothing" cycle, and celebrate the early progress that comes fast - clothes fitting better, energy rising, people saying you look healthier. Those early highs build belief and give you the proof that you can do this.

In the **Momentum phase**, confidence starts to stack. You hit major milestones you've struggled with for years - new strength numbers, visible physical changes, the lifestyle starting to feel natural. People notice. You notice. And you recover faster when challenges come up because you're no longer questioning whether you can succeed - you're focused on what's next.

In the **Identity phase**, mindset isn't something you think about - it's something you live. You're proud of what you've achieved and that you're maintaining it - something so many people struggle with. Your self-image has upgraded. You don't feel like someone "trying" anymore - you're the fit, strong, confident person you used to admire. And staying that person feels automatic, because your actions match who you are.

Get Your **FREE** Fat Loss Toolkit At: LesterKitching.com/ToolKit

The Power Of Sleep

Sleep is one of the most important tools for fat loss - yet it's usually the first thing sacrificed when life gets chaotic.

Late nights working, Netflix after the kids are finally asleep, scrolling to unwind - it's easy to justify.

But sleep isn't a luxury. It's a multiplier - it quietly amplifies everything else: training, nutrition, mindset, and energy.

When you cut back on sleep, your body pushes back.

Hunger hormones become unbalanced - making you crave high-calorie, high-carb foods.

Stress hormone levels rise, making fat loss harder and recovery slower.

And your decision-making - especially around food - gets worse.

You're not lazy or undisciplined - you're just tired.

Tired brains reach for easy wins: snacks, takeaways, skipped workouts, "I'll start again Monday."

Here's what most people never realise:

In a calorie deficit, sleep literally changes what your body burns.

If you're sleeping well and consistently getting around eight hours, your body burns a higher percentage of fat instead of muscle. The result? The toned, athletic look you want.

If you're consistently short on sleep, your body burns less fat and more muscle.

The result? You might still lose weight - but you'll lose a higher percentage of muscle, meaning less definition.

That's how much impact sleep really has.

Why Sleep Debt Sneaks Up On You

You might think losing an hour or two doesn't matter - but that sleep debt adds up fast.

Lose 90 minutes a night and that's over 10 hours of recovery gone each week - more than a full night's sleep.

You can push through for a while, but eventually, your body and mind hit a wall. That's usually when people think their plan "stopped working." In reality, they're just under-recovered. Their training feels harder, their cravings spike, and motivation nosedives.

For Parents And Busy Professionals

Let's be real - perfect sleep isn't always possible. You've got kids, work stress, late nights, early mornings.

So instead of chasing perfection, aim for consistency and make the most of recovery opportunities.

If you can't get eight hours straight, aim for six solid ones - then grab a short nap or an earlier night later in the week when you can.

How To Protect And Improve Your Sleep

- **Keep a consistent bedtime and wake-up window.** Stay within 30–60 minutes, even at weekends - it helps your body find a rhythm and makes falling asleep easier.

- **Set a "wind-down alarm."** When it goes off, put screens away, dim the lights, and let your brain switch off. Scrolling social media or watching a gripping box set keeps your brain wired when it should be winding down.

- **Keep caffeine early.** It stays in your system for 6–8 hours, so keep it before 2 pm.

- **Make your room a recovery zone.** Cool, dark, and quiet to give yourself the best chance of falling - and staying - asleep.

- **Use a notepad to brain dump.** If your brain won't switch off, write down what's on your mind and get it out of your head.

- **Have a hot shower or bath before bed.** The rise in body temperature, followed by the drop once you get out, signals to your body that it's time to sleep. It's a simple way to help you unwind and prepare for rest.

- **If you can't sleep, don't fight it.** If you've been tossing and turning for a while, get up and move to another room. Do something low-stimulation - read, stretch, or just sit quietly. After 20–30 minutes, head back to bed. This resets your mind and often helps you fall asleep faster than lying there frustrated.

- **Don't panic about bad nights - you'll have them.** It's the average that matters. One bad night doesn't ruin progress; one good week of sleep can totally change how you feel.

Sleep = Progress

You can't out-train or out-diet bad sleep.

It controls your hormones, recovery, hunger, and motivation.

When you improve your sleep, *everything else becomes easier* - your food choices, your training, your mood, and even your patience with your family.

Think of sleep as the foundation of your transformation.

When sleep is right, results aren't just faster - they're easier and more enjoyable.

Common Mistake To Avoid

Treating sleep as an afterthought.

Most people think they can "push through" tiredness and make up for it later - but that's like trying to out-train a bad diet. When sleep slips, hunger spikes, energy drops, and fat loss stalls. You start thinking your plan stopped working when, really, your body just hasn't had a chance to recover. Over time, this sleep debt builds up quietly and eats away at your motivation, performance, and results.

What To Do Instead

Protect your sleep like you protect your workouts.

Treat it as a non-negotiable part of your transformation - not an afterthought. Set a realistic routine, create an environment that helps you switch off, and aim for better sleep, not perfect sleep. You'll notice everything gets easier - effort feels lighter, cravings ease off, and results accelerate.

How Sleep Evolves Through The Phases

Sleep isn't something that changes phase-by-phase - it's a constant priority throughout your transformation.

In the **Ignite phase**, when you're building new routines and increasing your activity, you may notice you need more sleep as your body adapts.

Later, in the **Identity phase**, when you're stronger and lifting heavier, those demanding sessions - like squats or deadlifts - can leave you feeling more drained and in need of extra recovery.

But no matter where you are in your journey, high-quality sleep always makes everything else easier. That's why your approach to sleep should stay consistently prioritised - it supports progress at every level.

The Fallback Protocol

The Fallback Protocol acts as your pressure valve in the Transformation System - stopping chaos from undoing your progress.

It removes guilt, restores control, and gives you confidence that you can handle whatever life throws at you.

Follow it, and bad weeks don't turn into bad months. You won't have to rebuild from scratch every time life gets chaotic.

Instead, you stay in the game. And that's what separates people who *try* from people who transform.

Why Most People Fail During Chaos Weeks

When life gets messy, most people try to do more to make up for it. They double down on training, cut calories harder, or punish themselves for slipping.

That's the fast track to burnout.

You don't need to do more - you need to do less, better.

The Fallback Protocol is about stripping things back to the essentials that keep you steady. It's the minimum effective dose of structure that stops a tough week turning into a lost month and ultimately another abandoned fat loss attempt.

And this is important:

If you stick to your Fallback Protocol, you haven't failed - you've succeeded.

You're still in the fight when most people - even your former self - would have been taken out.

How The Fallback Protocol Works

When life gets messy - no time, high stress, zero bandwidth - the goal isn't to power through. It's to pull back strategically so you can recover, reset, and avoid spiralling backwards.

The Fallback Protocol gives you a simple structure for those tough weeks. You're not giving up - you're switching to maintenance mode: doing less, but still doing something.

Here's how it looks in practice:

- **Nutrition:** Priority number one. You can't control everything, but you *can* control your food choices. Stick to simple, satisfying meals to help you hold ground.

- **Training:** Optional. If you want to move, great - go for a walk, lift, or do something light. If you need a break, take it. You won't lose progress from a week or two of rest.

- **Sleep:** It's your recovery tool, not a luxury. Protect it as much as possible - an extra hour here and there makes a huge difference.

Even during the toughest weeks, holding ground *is* progress. Maintaining your weight, staying mindful around food, or moving in small ways all count - because the real setback isn't doing less, it's giving up.

Let's run through an example of how this might look:

You've got a packed work week - someone's away and you're picking up the slack. You've got to get in early, stay late, and stress levels are through the roof.

Realistically you've got very little time for the gym.

Your plan targets 3 sessions, but this week we dial it back. That's fine.

You skip workouts, stick to simple food choices, and grab healthy ready meals in the evening because you don't want to cook.

You get home, have your dinner, wind down with Netflix, and get to bed a little earlier instead.

No guilt. No frustration. No blame.

That's holding ground.

Now compare this to another person. Same situation.

They feel like they can't miss a session - "the plan says three workouts, I have to do them".

They get the first workout of the week done but now they're home late and need to cook dinner. The plan means they're cooking from scratch, and worst of all, it's something they don't really enjoy.

They eventually get into bed and doom scroll because they can't switch off.

The next training day comes and this time, they drive straight past the gym. No chance they are working out after the day they just had. They get home, and they've got to go through the hassle of cooking again, and once again, it's something they don't really want.

They grab the kids' chocolate bars and crisps while watching TV.

They wake up feeling guilty and ashamed - punishing themselves: "I always do this. Why can't I stick to anything?!"

After work, there's no chance they're going to the gym - they feel they'll need two workouts to catch up.

This time on the way home, they drive straight past the gym again, and because they cannot stand the thought of another dinner on their restrictive meal plan, they decide to grab a takeaway, grab more chocolate, and a bottle of wine to go with it.

Same situations.

Completely different outcomes.

One person used their Fallback Protocol and although it wasn't the best week, they've held ground and when normality returns, they're feeling good and ready to push again.

The other person has crashed out on their fat loss transformation. They're crushed and give up entirely. And over the next 2 months, regain all the weight lost.

Exactly the same situations, but completely different outcomes.

Common Mistake To Avoid

Trying to force perfection during imperfect weeks.

When life gets hectic, many people panic and cling harder to their plan - pushing through exhaustion, skipping recovery, and trying to "make up" for missed workouts or meals. It comes from good intentions but leads to burnout, guilt, and eventually, giving up altogether. When life stops fitting the plan, they assume they've failed and spiral backward.

What To Do Instead

Adapt, don't abandon.

When stress or time is high, lower the bar instead of walking away. Focus on the few controllable things - simple meals, decent sleep, and doing something you enjoy. Training can wait. The goal during tough weeks isn't progress - it's preservation. Hold your ground, ride the wave, and reset when life steadies. That's how you stay consistent long-term - not by doing everything perfectly, but by never quitting completely.

The Power Of Holding Ground

The biggest mistake people make is believing progress is linear - and that's normal. There will be weeks, both in and out of your control, where you simply hold ground.

Progress is built in the moments you could quit - but don't. Maintaining instead of taking three steps back.

Every time you stay in the game during a rough week, you strengthen your identity as someone who follows through. And you prove to yourself that you can do this long term.

It's one thing to succeed during the good weeks. Succeeding during tough weeks gives you a massive confidence boost - even if you've tried and failed in the past.

When you zoom out after six months, a year, five years - you'll see those "maintenance weeks" for what they really are: key moments in your transformation.

Your Personal Fallback Plan

I build this with every client before it's needed - so when chaos hits, they already know what to do.

Here's how to create yours:

1. **Write down your "worst week" scenario.** What does it usually look like for you? No time, no energy, high stress?

2. **List the one or two things you *can* still do** in that week. Focus heavily on nutrition. You can lose weight without exercise - not without nutrition.

3. **Define success for that week.** It's not "did I make progress?" - it's "did I hold ground?"

That becomes your personal Fallback Protocol.

And the moment you start using it, you'll realise something powerful:

You can't fail anymore - only pause progress when needed until life settles - then pick up right where you left off, without guilt or shame.

That's what long-term consistency really looks like.

That's what makes this time different from every other attempt.

How The Fallback Protocol Evolves Through The Phases

In the **Ignite phase**, the Fallback Protocol is your safety net. You're still building your habits and rhythm, so knowing there's a backup plan in place removes pressure and keeps you from spiralling the first time life gets chaotic. You're learning the mindset shift from "all or nothing" to "always something."

In **Momentum**, the Fallback Protocol becomes your stabiliser. You've built a routine and you're pushing progress, but busy weeks will still happen. Instead of losing confidence or slipping backwards, you use your fallback plan to hold ground - you stay in control even when life isn't.

By the **Identity phase**, the Fallback Protocol becomes instinctive. You no longer panic when time gets tight or stress spikes - you automatically switch to a simpler version of your routine. You trust that holding ground is progress. It's part of the identity shift: you don't quit anymore, you adjust.

The Real Reason You'll Stick To It

Here's the truth: this book isn't about quick fixes or shortcuts - but if there's one thing that comes close to a cheat code, it's accountability.

At the start of your transformation, accountability gives you the push you need when motivation fades and old habits creep in.

Later on, it becomes your reflection tool - helping you stay honest, make smart adjustments, and keep moving when progress slows.

Think about work. There are mornings you'd love to stay in bed, skip the commute, or take the day off - but you still show up.

Why? Because there's accountability. There are expectations, deadlines, and people who count on you. You don't rely on motivation to go to work; you rely on commitment.

Now imagine if work were optional - "just show up when you feel motivated." How many people would show up five days a week? Very few.

Motivation alone isn't reliable.

Your fat-loss journey works the same way.

Without accountability, it's easy to skip workouts, relax your nutrition, and tell yourself you'll "start again Monday."

With accountability, you **raise your standards** - most of us fight much harder to avoid failing in public than in private. That's the difference between consistency and quitting.

Accountability isn't guilt or pressure - it's awareness.

It helps you zoom out and stay aligned when life gets messy. Just like talking a problem through with a partner or a friend, accountability gives you perspective when you can't see it yourself.

Challenges will come. Having someone - or even a structured process - to talk things through helps you respond intelligently instead of emotionally. That often decides whether you're back on track tomorrow, or you lose another month to frustration.

That's the power of accountability: **it keeps you in the game.**

And while self-accountability is powerful, **third-party accountability** - having a coach, mentor, or supportive group - takes it to another level.

It removes the emotion from your decisions, keeps you honest when you'd otherwise talk yourself out of action, and gives you expert eyes and objective feedback you simply can't get on your own.

When someone else is in your corner - tracking your progress, helping you problem-solve, and holding you to your word - you perform at a higher level - every single time.

The Check-In Ritual

Reading about accountability is one thing - using it is what creates change. Your check-in ritual is how you do that: a regular pause to reflect, realign, and reset for the week ahead. It doesn't take long - ten minutes can completely change your week.

Ways to run it:

- A quick weekly reflection on wins, challenges, and next steps.
- A short data check - weight trend, training frequency, step count.
- A monthly review with your coach or accountability partner to fine-tune your approach.
- A simple tracker - apps or marking your calendar each time you've worked out.

Accountability doesn't punish you when things go wrong - it guides you back when they do. It's the glue that keeps effort, structure, and motivation working together.

Don't Stop The Thing That Got You There

Here's where many people go wrong - after hitting their goal, they remove the very structure that got them there. They stop tracking, stop checking in, and bit by bit, old patterns creep back.

You don't need intense accountability forever - but you do need **some**.

Light accountability keeps you aware of early slippage and reminds you what matters.

That might look like:

- A brief weekly or fortnightly self-review.
- A deeper review with your coach every 30 days.
- Setting a fresh mini-goal to stay sharp.

Don't see accountability as pressure - see it as protection. It stops you letting yourself off on the hard days and helps you find solutions when things feel off.

In the end, accountability is what turns good intentions into consistent action - and consistent action into lasting transformation.

Common Mistake To Avoid

Trying to rely on motivation alone - or assuming you can stay accountable without any outside help. Motivation fades, and without external accountability, discipline often goes with it.

What To Do Instead

Build layers of accountability. Do self-check-ins, but add third-party accountability - a coach, mentor, or community - if you're serious about staying consistent, supported, and at your best when motivation's low.

How Accountability Evolves Through The Phases

In the **Ignite phase**, accountability gives you the push you need. Motivation is high but fragile, so having someone or something to check in with keeps you moving when the excitement fades or life gets in the way. It helps you build early consistency and belief quickly.

In **Momentum**, accountability becomes your anchor. Progress slows, life distractions creep in, and old habits try to return. Regular check-ins keep you honest, focused, and adjusting the plan instead of abandoning it. It stops a dip in motivation becoming a full derailment.

By the **Identity phase**, accountability becomes light but essential. You don't need someone watching your every move - but you still benefit from structure and occasional check-ins to ensure you stay sharp and protect the results you've worked hard for. You're no longer accountable because you fear slipping - you're accountable because it supports who you now are.

Get Your **FREE** Fat Loss Toolkit At: **LesterKitching.com/ToolKit**

PART 4

This Time Really Is Different

This Time Really Is Different

If you've made it this far, you're not just interested anymore - you're committed to finally achieving what you've spent so long working toward. Congratulations!

You've done what most people never do - you've slowed down long enough to understand what actually works. Instead of bouncing from random workouts and crash diets, you've learned the process of your transformation and built a system that fits your life - even on the tough days.

And that matters.

Because every failed attempt before now wasn't a lack of willpower - it was a lack of structure.

You didn't have the Transformation Framework to understand the journey - and the emotions, challenges, and pitfalls that come with real life.

You didn't have the Transformation System to guide your actions - to get results without starving yourself, restrictive diets, or forcing yourself through workouts you hate.

But now you do.

Now you've got the tools, the understanding, and the roadmap to finally break the cycle.

No more guilt. No more perfection-chasing. No more starting over every Monday.

You know how to set goals that light you up, and how to stay aligned with them so you have more good days than bad ones.

You know the key principles for eating in a way that you enjoy, can stick to, and get results.

You know how to get that toned, athletic look without spending all your time in the gym.

You know how to adapt when life gets busy - the Fallback Protocol.

And you know the importance of accountability - something we all need to stay consistent when energy dips.

This isn't about being perfect anymore.

The old you was waiting for the right time. The new you knows the time is now. And you've got everything you need to make it all work in the real world.

From here, it's about taking action - one step at a time.

Every small win counts. Every bit of progress adds up. And every time you show up, you're proving to yourself that this time really *is* different.

This is your turning point - not another plan, but a permanent shift.

A transformation that fits the real world.

Built to last.

What Happens Next

1. Download Your Fat Loss For The Real World Toolkit

Grab the free resources that go with this book - simple, practical tools to help you turn what you've learned into results.

Inside, you'll find templates, planners, and guides designed to make your journey easier, clearer, and more consistent.

To download your free toolkit head to:

LesterKitching.com/Toolkit

2. Attend a Live Fat Loss For The Real World Workshop

If you're serious about getting results and want to keep building on what you've learned, I would love to see you at one of my live workshops.

I host these regularly, both online and in person, and each one focuses on a key area of transformation.

These are small-group sessions - intentionally kept that way so you can ask questions, share experiences, and get direct, personal coaching from me.

They're completely free to attend, and spaces go fast - so if you'd like to join the next one, head over to:

LesterKitching.com/Workshop

Get Your **FREE** Fat Loss Toolkit At: **LesterKitching.com/ToolKit**

Final Words

Thank you for reading this book. I hope it's just the start of our journey together - as you finally achieve your fat loss goal without turning your life upside down to get there. I know how impactful that would be. Not just for you, but for your family and friends.

And I really hope that I get to meet you in-person or virtually at one of my upcoming workshops.

Thank you, and speak to you soon,

Lester Kitching

Email: **lester@lesterkitching.com**

Website: **LesterKitching.com**

Instagram: **@LesterKitching**

Printed in Dunstable, United Kingdom